THE NEW BOOK OF
the Art of

LIVING

by

WILFERD A. PETERSON

A new series of twenty-seven essays

Introduction by William I. Nichols

SIMON AND SCHUSTER · NEW YORK

NINTH PRINTING

Quotation from The Art Spirit *by Robert Henri*
reprinted by permission of J. B. Lippincott Company.

Library of Congress Catalog Card Number: 63-16024
Manufactured in the United States of America
Typography by The Photo-Composing Room, New York
Printed by United Lithographing Corp., New York

*To my wife, Ruth, in gratitude
for her help and inspiration*

INTRODUCTION

THIS IS *the second collection of essays on the Art of Living by Wilferd A. Peterson and, like the first, is published in response to popular demand. The first, issued in 1961, was based on a series of essays which appeared in* This Week *Magazine, and more than half a million readers were so impressed that they asked for the book. This new collection also includes a number of essays published in* This Week. *From the initial response we know that this second book will meet with a similar enthusiastic welcome.*

I mention this response not in a spirit of boastfulness but because it seems to confirm the author's central gift, which is to speak to people in terms of their deepest wants in today's anxious world.

For, no matter what the cynics and skeptics may say, man does not *live by bread alone. This is something which Wilferd Peterson understands and believes passionately. His whole creed is summed up in these words from his opening essay: "Man alone, of all the creatures of earth, can change his own pattern. Man alone is architect of his destiny."*

At a time when others despair, he approaches this challenge of life with a deep sense of awe, wonder, faith and hope. And by sharing this spirit, he gives strength and new purpose to the millions who read his words.

WILLIAM I. NICHOLS
Editor and Publisher
THIS WEEK *Magazine*

≶ Art when really understood is the province of every human being.

≶ It is simply a question of doing things, anything, well. It is not an outside extra thing.

≶ When the artist is alive in any person, whatever his kind of work may be, he becomes an inventive, searching, daring, self-expressing creature. He becomes interesting to other people. He disturbs, upsets, enlightens, and he opens ways for a better understanding.

—ROBERT HENRI
in *The Art Spirit*

CONTENTS

❧

THE ART OF
Changing Yourself

L IFE IS constantly pounding you from the outside with millions of hammer blows, but you have the last word as to how those blows will change you.

Man alone, of all the creatures of earth, can change his own pattern. Man alone is architect of his destiny.

William James declared that the greatest revolution in his generation was the discovery that human beings, by changing the inner attitudes of their minds, can change the outer aspects of their lives.

History and literature are full of examples of the miracle of inner change—Paul on the Damascus Road . . . Ernest and the Great Stone Face . . . the hunchback prince, of the Persian story, who became straight and tall by standing each day before a statue of himself made straight . . .

You cannot climb uphill by thinking downhill thoughts. If your world is gloomy and hopeless, it is because *you* are gloomy and hopeless. *You must change your mind to change your world.*

Change demands self-discipline. Command yourself and make yourself do what needs to be done.

8

Change requires the substituting of new habits for old. You mold your character and your future by your thoughts and acts.

Change can be advanced by associating with men and women with whom you can walk among the stars. Meet, mingle and make friends with those who have the upward urge.

Change can be inspired by selecting your own spiritual ancestors from among the great of all the ages. You can practice the kindliness of Lincoln, the devotion of Schweitzer, the vision of Franklin . . .

Change can be achieved by changing your environment. Let go of lower things and reach for the higher. Surround yourself with the best in books, music and art. Listen to the greatest speakers. Hang on the walls of your home portraits of the men you most admire.

Change can be realized through *conscious evolution*. Moment by moment, day by day, concentrate on becoming the man you want to be.

Change can be accomplished most of all through the power of prayer, because with God all things are possible.

THE ART OF
America

A MERICA is a unique way of life symbolic of the creative arts.

America provides the brushes, oils, pigments, and the canvas on which you can paint your life as you want it to be. You choose your own colors, your own form, design and pattern.

America is any tune you want to play with fife and drum, fiddle or horn to establish the beat and rhythm of the upward march to high goals.

America is a book in which you set down your life by the way you live it. You are the principal character. You *live* your own biography. You are free to be hero or villain, great or mediocre.

America is a stage, and the role you play in the drama of life is up to you.

America is a sports arena, and the rules are written so everyone has a chance to win.

America is an engineering achievement, a bridge over which you can cross the chasm of despair.

America is an architecture with which you can build the tower of your dreams.

America is a sculptor's hammer and chisel with which you can fashion yourself into the man you aim to become.

America is an art of living through which you can reach higher, think bigger, grow greater and live deeper than anywhere else on earth. ✹

THE ART OF
Worship

OUTER SYMBOLS create the atmosphere and mood of worship—the altar, the cross, the candles, the stained-glass windows; the silent sanctuary before the service begins . . .

In cathedral or cottage, the art of worship is an *inner adventure;* it is the personal practice of the presence of God.

It is meditation and prayer expressing the soul's sincere desire.

It is resting our weary hearts and minds on the Everlasting Arms.

It is emptying and cleansing our minds of fear and worry, jealousy and envy that God may fill the vacuum with His goodness.

It is being quiet and relaxed that we may experience the inflow of the peace that passes all understanding.

It is counting our many blessings and giving thanks for the power to grow, to serve, to conquer ourselves and to discover the sublime values of the life of the spirit.

It is the inspiring realization that this is God's world, that all life pulsates with God's eternal purpose and that we are a part of the divine pattern and plan.

It is envisioning, high and lifted up, all that is heroic, great, good and beautiful in our common life.

It is realigning our lives again with the laws and principles of God, that we may move forward, with our brothers, on the pathway of the King.

It is the renewing of our noblest dreams and aspirations that we may rise above defeat, failure and discouragement and have another try at making the most of our lives.

It is climbing to the spiritual mountaintop of conscious oneness with God that we may light again the candles of our spirits and return as *new men* to the valley and our work.

THE ART OF
Keeping Christmas

HOW CAN we best keep Christmas? How can we best defeat the little bit of Scrooge in all of us and experience the glory of the Great Day?

By sinking the shafts of our spirits deep beneath the sparkling tinsel of the surface of Christmas and renewing within us the radiance of the inner meaning of the season.

By following the Star on an inward journey to Bethlehem to stand again in awe and wonder before the Babe in a Manger.

By rediscovering the faith and simplicity of a little child, for of such is the Kingdom of Heaven.

By being still and listening to the angels sing within our hearts.

By quietly evaluating our lives according to the Master's standards as set forth in the Sermon on the Mount.

By reaffirming the supremacy of the spirit in man's conquest of himself.

By rededicating ourselves to the Master's ideals of Peace, Brotherhood and Good Will.

By resolving to *give ourselves away* to others in love, joy and devotion.

By using the light of Christmas to guide us through the darkness of the coming year, refusing to go back to the dim kerosene lamps of the spirit when the brilliant electricity of Christmas is available to show us the way. ✤

THE ART OF
Freedom

F REEDOM is a *personal thing*.

Freedom is an *open door,* but you must walk through it.

Freedom is a *ladder,* but you must climb it.

Freedom doesn't mean that you can do what you please, but it does mean that there isn't anything holding you back from striving to make your finest dreams come true.

Freedom is yours now, this very minute, and what you do with it is up to you. You can aim at the highest goal.

Freedom is an invitation to be creative—to paint, sing, carve, write, build, according to your heart's desire.

Freedom is the opportunity to dedicate your life to the service of others. You can follow your gleam wherever it leads.

Freedom is your right to be yourself, to make mistakes, to fail and try again. No failure is final; freedom always gives you another chance.

Freedom is a blessing to be shared. The fruits of freedom depend upon the interaction of the thoughts, ideas and ideals of men.

Freedom is a wide horizon gleaming with promise. The only chains and shackles you must break are within you. You practice the art of freedom when you make the most of all that freedom offers.

Freedom is God's gift to you. "Where the spirit of the Lord is, there is liberty," wrote Saint Paul.

Thank God for your freedom. It is your key to an inspiring future.

THE ART OF
Loafing

"I LOAF and invite my soul," sang the poet Walt Whitman.

The art of loafing is following the philosophy of the vagabond who said, "I turn my back to the wind." It is drifting and dreaming and opening yourself to the inflow of peace and tranquillity.

It is easing the pounding of your heart by the quieting of your mind.

It is relaxing the tension of your body with the music of the singing streams that live in your memory.

It is reminding yourself of the fable of the Hare and the Tortoise that you may know that the race is not always to the swift, that there is more to life than increasing its speed.

It is slowing down to look at a flower, to chat with a friend, to pat a dog, to read a few lines from a book.

It is using your hands to plane a board, paint a picture or plant a garden. It is experiencing the adventure of a change of pace.

It is loafing with one eye open for the flashes of light that may illumine your mind with the answers you seek.

It is sinking the shafts of your thoughts deep into the eternal well of God's wisdom. It is listening within to the truth that makes men free.

When problems arise, when pressures mount, follow the wise rule Admiral Byrd used when his ship was locked in the ice of the Antarctic: "Give wind and tide a chance to change."

Pause and still your mind. Go to the window and look up at the stars.

The art of loafing can add dimension and scope to your life. It can change your perspective and renew your spirit. Just as rests and pauses are a part of great music, so are they also a part of *great living*.

He who finds time to loaf is a wise man. ✳

THE ART OF
Getting Along

SOONER OR LATER a man, if he is wise, discovers that life is a mixture of good days and bad, victory and defeat, give and take.

He learns that a man's size is often measured by the size of the thing it takes to get his goat . . . that the conquest of petty irritations is vital to success.

He learns that he who loses his temper usually loses.

He learns that carrying a chip on his shoulder is the quickest way to get into a fight.

He learns that buck-passing acts as a boomerang.

He learns that carrying tales and gossip about others is the easiest way to become unpopular.

He learns that everyone is human and that he can help to make the day happier for others by smiling and saying, "Good morning!"

He learns that giving others a mental lift by showing appreciation and praise is the best way to lift his own spirits.

He learns that the world will not end when he fails or makes an error; that there is always another day and another chance.

He learns that listening is frequently more important than talking, and that he can often make a friend by letting the other fellow tell *his* troubles.

He learns that all men have burnt toast for breakfast now and then and that he shouldn't let their grumbling get him down.

He learns that people are not any more difficult to get along with in one place than another and that "getting along" depends about ninety-eight per cent on his own behavior.

THE ART OF
Peace

Lord make me an instrument of Thy peace . . ." Thus begins the inspired prayer of Saint Francis of Assisi. Peace can be achieved only *through people!*

World-wide peace and peace in our little worlds of home, family, office, industry, community . . . depend upon each one of us putting into action the art of peace ∴ . .

Peace is God on both sides of the table in a conference.

It is putting the power of good will to work.

It is sanity, maturity and common sense in human relationships.

It is open-mindedness. It is a willingness to listen as well as to speak. It is looking at both sides of a situation objectively.

It is patience. It means keeping our tempers and rising above petty irritations. It is counting to ten and avoiding hasty and impulsive decisions.

It is having the courage and humility to admit mistakes and to take the blame when we are wrong.

It is tact. Tact has been defined as the ability to pull the stinger of a bee without getting stung.

It is vision. It is taking the long look. It is being willing to give up individual advantages for the common good.

It is straight thinking. It is recognizing that iron curtains *are not metal, but mental,* and that they are woven of fear, prejudice and mistrust.

It is a quality of the heart as well as the head. It is a warmth, an enthusiasm, a magnetism that reaches out and draws people together in understanding and love.

It is a mighty faith in the goodness of God and the potential greatness of man.

THE ART OF
Walking

W ALKING exercises the *whole man*.

Walking exercises the body. It gives the arms and legs a workout. It stimulates the flow of blood; expands the lungs. It is gentle and relaxing.

Walking exercises the mind. It shakes up the brain cells. It fills them with oxygen; drives out the cobwebs. A famous scientist says he does his best thinking on the two miles of sidewalk between his home and his office.

Walking exercises the emotions. It gives you a chance to observe and enjoy the world. Open your eyes to beauty. See the homes, the trees, the gardens. See the shining faces of little children. Listen for church chimes, singing birds and the laughter of happy people.

Walking uplifts the spirit. Breathe out the poisons of tension, stress and worry; breathe in the power of God. Send forth little silent prayers of good will toward those you meet.

Walk with the sense of being a part of a vast universe. Consider the thousands of miles of earth beneath your feet; think of the limitless expanse of space above your head. Walk in awe, wonder and humility.

Walk at all times of day. In the early morning when the world is just waking up. Late at night under the stars. Along a busy city street at noontime.

Walk in all kinds of weather. Experience the glory of earth coming back to life in springtime; the warming rays of the sun in summer; the zest of October's bright-blue weather; the rugged desolation of winter. Walk in the rain and in a blizzard.

Walk alone mostly, but if with a companion, choose one who knows the secret of quietness.

Walk for fun and adventure, for health and inspiration.

And when you go for a walk remember these words by Elbert Hubbard: "Carry your chin in and the crown of your head high. We are gods in the chrysalis."

THE ART OF
Empathy

Someone has made the wise observation that a man wrapped up in himself makes a very small package. Such a man is *self-centered*. The dimensions of his life are dwarfed and limited.

The practice of empathy makes a man *other-centered*. Through the power of his creative imagination empathy enables him to project himself into the consciousness of others that he may know how they think and how they feel.

Sympathy merely mirrors another man's trouble; empathy discovers the causes of the trouble with the searchlight of insight.

Through empathy a man comes to appreciate another person's feelings without becoming so emotionally involved that his judgment is affected.

Through empathy a man learns not to judge others in terms of his own personal interests, likes and dislikes, but in terms of what life means to *them*.

The Sioux Indians expressed the attitude of empathy when they prayed, "Great Spirit, help us never to judge another until we have walked for two weeks in his moccasins."

Through empathy a man may closely identify himself with anyone he may wish to understand. He may seek inspiration from the gifted, the victorious, the happy. He may develop a deep comprehension of the problems of the blind, the crippled, the sorrowing and the defeated.

Through empathy a man may become all men under all conditions of stress and difficulty.

Empathy is the key to leadership. It unlocks the dreams in the hearts of men so the leader can help to make those dreams come true.

Empathy helps to create harmony in the home. Family members may play the roles of each other. For instance, the father can play the part of the son and the son the part of the father, that each may learn to know and appreciate the feelings of the other.

Practicing the art of empathy will enlarge a man's life.

It will broaden his humanity, expand his understanding and inspire tolerance and forbearance, compassion and forgiveness.

THE ART OF
Taking Time to Live

To GET the most out of life we must take time to live as well as to make a living. We must practice the art of filling our moments with enriching experiences that will give new meaning and depth to our lives.

We should take time for good books; time to absorb the thoughts of poets and philosophers, seers and prophets.

Time for music that washes away from the soul the dust of everyday life.

Time for friendships; time for talks by the fire and walks beneath the stars.

Time for children that we may find again the Kingdom of Heaven within our hearts.

Time for laughter; time for letting go and filling the heart with mirth.

Time for travel; time for pilgrimage and festival, for shrine and exhibit, for rockbound coast and desert, mountain and plain.

Time for nature; time for flower gardens, trees, birds and sunsets.

Time to love and be loved, for love is the greatest thing in the world.

Time for people; time for the interplay of personalities and the interchange of ideas.

Time for solitude; time to be quiet and alone and to look within.

Time to give of ourselves, our talents, abilities, devotions, convictions, that we may contribute to the onward march of man.

Time for worship; time for opening our lives to God's infinite springs of vitality, that we may live more abundantly.

In all ways let us make our moments glow with life. Let us pray as did Matthew Arnold: "Calm, calm me more, nor let me die, before I have begun to live."

THE ART OF
Perspective

SAID the Emperor Marcus Aurelius: *"Live as on a mountain."*

Mountain heights cause spirits to soar. How can one be mentally small who associates with the magnificent bigness of mountains?

The mountaintop man lives on an invisible mountain of the mind.

His perspective is broad, his outlook far-reaching.

His spirit towers above the storms of life.

His mind is lifted up, above doubt, cynicism and despair.

His vision is high above the fog of petty things.

He looks beyond the obstacles to the promised land of to-morrow.

He sees the rainbows while little men battle with phantom shadows in the valley.

He sees the sun in the east while valley-dwellers burn their tiny lamps in darkness.

His head is in the clouds, but his feet are bedded in the solid rock of Fact and Reason.

He takes the risks; he dares the sky.

He lives with the stars of his ideals, and although he may never grasp them he keeps reaching toward them.

BEING just an ordinary human being wandering along the pathway of life, I've evolved this simple philosophy to guide me:

To affirm that I am proud to be a member of the human race; to recognize that, regardless of color, class or creed, man's destiny is my destiny, and that only as we learn to live together will we move forward together.

To accept life as it is and to go along with it, bravely trying to change what needs to be changed and serenely adapting myself to what cannot be changed.

To realize that no experience in human life is alien to me and that my responsibility is to meet whatever happens to me with fortitude and courage.

To admit that, being human, I am bound to make mistakes, but to make as few as possible and to try to avoid making the same mistake twice.

To recognize the frailties and foibles of human nature and to try to be everlastingly patient, forgiving and understanding.

To promptly forget slights and insults and to hope that others will not hold against me the winged arrows that may in anger or irritation escape my lips.

To share my courage and hope with others and keep my fears, heartaches and disappointments to myself.

To go my way quietly and humbly and not worry too much about mysteries I cannot explain. To do my best here and now and let the future take care of itself.

To be grateful for the precious gift of life with its limitless possibilities. To glory in the power of human beings to rise to great heights and to outdo themselves in miraculous works. To find inspiration in the words of Browning: "A man's reach should exceed his grasp or what's a heaven for?"

To understand that the goodness of God can be known only through human goodness; that when I express the highest and best I express God.

To confront the inevitable fact that I share with all human beings a common end: that someday Death, the kind old nurse, will rock us all to sleep, so we should help each other while we can.

To admit that, being human, I often fail to live up to my own philosophy, but to keep trying nevertheless.

Progress

THE ART OF progress is the story of man's relentless determination to improve his condition.

Man, genus Homo, held back by tyrants, dark ages, ignorance, fear, economic disaster and war, yet ultimately breaking the shackles and marching forward to the music of his greater destiny.

Caves, sod huts, log cabins, hammers and nails and frame buildings, brick on brick, then steel girders swinging through space and skyscrapers against the skyline.

Rough-hewn wooden wheels, faster-moving wheels of wagons, gasoline buggies, steam engines, modern automobiles and wheels lifted from the earth by the wings of planes.

Strange hieroglyphics carved on the walls of ancient temples, discovery of paper; monks in the monasteries copying the Holy Bible with quill pens; Gutenberg and movable type, and the roar of a million printing presses.

Slavery and serfdom, whipping posts and stocks, then the awakening of the human spirit and the vision of freedom and the brotherhood of man.

Galileo peering into the night sky with an iron pipe for a telescope, and then a giant lens that looks a billion light-years into space.

The Wright brothers, airborne for only ten seconds and one hundred feet on the first flight, and now man in orbit around the earth.

Smoke signals, tapping of a telegraph key, voice over a wire, radio, television and Telstar in the heavens.

Crude, agonizing primitive surgery without anesthesia, and now the magic of deep sleep while miracles are performed.

Columbus crossing the Atlantic in the forty-two-foot ship the *Niña,* Fulton and his steamboat, floating cities plowing the deep, and jet planes making the world a neighborhood.

Candles, oil lamps, Franklin flying his kite into a thunder cloud, and Edison illuminating the world with the first electric light.

Clubs, bows and arrows, fire and catapults, gunpowder, artillery, bombing planes, and then the splitting of the atom making man a titan with the power to destroy civilization or to take a great leap forward in human progress.

Man delayed by ten thousand detours, yet rising after each fall, always building stronger and higher the things he destroys and triumphantly marching forward under the go light of progress, leaving giant footprints on the sands of time.

THE ART OF
Renewal

YOUR BIRTHDAY is the beginning of your own *personal* new year.

Your first birthday was a beginning, and each new birthday is a chance to *begin again,* to start over, to take a new grip on life . . .

It is a time to consider the wisdom of Socrates: "The un-examined life is not worth living." It is a time to re-evaluate your past as a guide to your future.

It is a time to remind yourself that "saints are sinners who keep on trying."

It is a time to toss old hatreds, resentments, grudges and fears into the wastebasket of life; a time to forgive and forget, a time to stretch your soul.

It is a time to list the things you have left undone and to do something about them: the visits you've failed to make, the words unspoken, the letters unwritten, the tasks unfinished.

It is a time to dust off your dreams and shine up your ideals.

It is a time to browse through the precious old books that have meant the most to you that you may rediscover illuminating phrases and sentences to light your pathway into the future.

It is a time to give thanks to God, and to man, for the riches that have been poured into your life; a time to appreciate anew the beauty and wonder of the world.

It is a time to rededicate your life to those things which are enduring, recognizing with William James that "the great use of life is to spend it on something that will outlast it."

It is a time to resolve to *add life to your years,* for as Philip James Bailey points out, "he most lives who thinks most, feels the noblest, acts the best."

THE ART OF
Listening

THE KEY to the art of listening is *selectivity*. You stand guard at the ear-gateway to your mind, heart and spirit. You decide what you will accept....

Listen to the good. Tune your ears to love, hope and courage. Tune out gossip, fear and resentment.

Listen to the beautiful. Relax to the music of the masters; listen to the symphony of nature—hum of the wind in the treetops, bird songs, thundering surf.

Listen with your *eyes*. Imaginatively listen to the sounds in a poem, a novel, a picture.

Listen critically. Mentally challenge assertions, ideas, philosophies. Seek the truth with an open mind.

Listen with patience. Do not hurry the other person. Show him the courtesy of listening to what he has to say, no matter how much you may disagree. You may learn something.

Listen with your heart. Practice empathy when you listen; put yourself in the other person's place and try to hear his problems in your heart.

Listen for growth. Be an inquisitive listener. Ask questions. Everyone has something to say which will help you to grow.

Listen creatively. Listen carefully for ideas or the germs of ideas. Listen for hints or clues which will spark creative projects.

Listen to yourself. Listen to your deepest yearnings, your highest aspirations, your noblest impulses. Listen to the better man within you.

Listen with depth. Be still and meditate. Listen with the ear of intuition for the inspiration of the Infinite.

≥≥≥≥≥≥≥≥≥≥≥≥≥≥≥≥≥≥≥≥≥≥≥≥≥

THE ART OF
Imagination

I MAGINATION," said Einstein, "is more powerful than knowledge."

Imagination enlarges vision, stretches the mind, challenges the impossible. Without imagination, thought comes to a halt!

You awaken your imagination through the driving power of *curiosity* and *discontent*.

You *light up* your imagination by stoking your mental fires through the senses—eyes, ears, nose, muscles, skin. You spur your imagination by giving it abundant data with which to work.

You take time for dreams and fantasy, knowing that only as you become as open and receptive as a little child, shall you enter into the Kingdom of Ideas.

You rub shoulders with men, watching for the creative sparks that generate new concepts and approaches.

You learn from that great master of imagination Thomas Alva Edison, who when asked the secret of his inventive genius replied, "I listen from within."

You use your imagination to look at everything with fresh eyes, as though you had just come forth from a dark tunnel into the light of day.

Your imagination becomes for you a magic lamp with which to explore the darkness of the unknown that you may chart new paths to old goals.

You recognize the reality of facts, but you use your imagination to penetrate beneath them and to project your thought beyond them in your search for creative answers to problems.

Imagination "stirs up the gift of God in thee." Through your imagination you touch and express the inspiration of the Infinite.

Imagination, in the words of Shakespeare, "gives to airy nothing a local habitation and a name." You reach into the heavens to grasp an idea, then you bring it down to earth and make it work.

THE ART OF
Power

REALLY great men," wrote Ruskin, "have the feeling that the greatness is not in them but *through* them."

You stand at the pinnacle of life, and you can be a channel for mighty streams of power.

The art of power is the opening of yourself to all the sources of power at your command . . .

The power of wisdom. All the great thoughts of the thinkers of all the ages are yours to use. You are the heir of more accumulated knowledge and experience than man has *ever before possessed. You are standing on the shoulders of giants!*

The power of thought. All great living must spring, like a fountain, from within your mind. The quality of the thoughts you think will determine your destiny.

The power of the heart. Emotional drive is the mark of the dynamic achievers. When you put your heart in your work, even so-called impossibilities become possible.

The power of a dream. Great dreams become obsessions which will not be denied. If you are willing to pay the price, you can make your dream come true. "Now and then, not often," wrote Emerson, "a man forgets himself into immortality."

The power of people. Character and ideals are catching. When you associate with men who aspire to the highest and best, you expose yourself to the qualities that make men great.

The power of the spirit. Even Napoleon came to recognize that the spirit is the greatest power of all. After his attempted military conquest of the world had failed he wrote: "There are only two powers in the world, the spirit and the sword. In the long run the sword will always be conquered by the spirit."

The power of the Infinite. Powerful forces come to your aid when you keep in tune with the Infinite. "When we pray," declared the scientist Alexis Carrel, "we link ourselves with the inexhaustible power that spins the universe."

You are a divinely appointed guardian of all the powers man has evolved since time began. It is your duty to use these powers for man's continued growth and development and to pass them on renewed and enlarged to those who will follow you. ✂️

HAPPINESS in marriage is not something that just happens. A good marriage must be created. In the art of marriage the *little things* are the *big things* . . .

It is never being too old to hold hands.

It is remembering to say, "I love you," at least once each day.

It is never going to sleep angry.

It is at no time taking the other for granted; the courtship shouldn't end with the honeymoon, it should continue through all the years.

It is having a mutual sense of values and common objectives; it is standing together facing the world.

It is forming a circle of love that gathers in the whole family.

It is doing things for each other, not in the attitude of duty or sacrifice, but in the spirit of joy.

It is speaking words of appreciation and demonstrating gratitude in thoughtful ways.

It is not expecting the husband to wear a halo or the wife to have the wings of an angel. It is not looking for perfection in each other. It is cultivating flexibility, patience, understanding and a sense of humor.

It is having the capacity to forgive and forget.

It is giving each other an atmosphere in which each can grow.

It is finding room for the things of the spirit. It is a common search for the good and the beautiful.

It is establishing a relationship as counseled by Louis K. Anspacher, in which "the independence is equal, the dependence is mutual and the obligation is reciprocal."

It is not only marrying the right partner, it is *being* the right partner.

It is discovering what marriage can be, at its best, as expressed in the words Mark Twain used in a tribute to his wife: "Wherever she was, there was Eden."

THE ART OF
Maturity

THE DISTILLED experience of many men has resulted in discoveries like these about the art of mature living . . .

That life is too short to be wasted in hatred, revenge, fault-finding, prejudice, intolerance and destruction.

That only the affirmative approach inspires progress. We should follow the wise advice of Charles W. Eliot and "cultivate a calm nature, expectant of good."

That our basic direction should always be toward *wholeness* of life. The great life is built on deep and enduring values. Like a giant tree, we should grow from within.

That no outstanding work is done alone. Miracles can be achieved when we don't care who gets the credit.

That we should not dodge reality or turn our backs on situations that must be faced. Private bravery is the price of personal victory.

That it is never wise to become too elated or too discouraged. As Robert Louis Stevenson suggested, we should strive to "go on in fortune and misfortune like a clock during a thunderstorm."

That a few troubles and a little pain are good for us and help us to grow. We should not complain that the rosebush has thorns but should rejoice because it bears roses.

That time is the great healer of hurts, sorrows and disappointments. When one door closes another will open if we don't lose heart.

That it is wiser to judge a man by how he lives than by what he says.

That moderation in all things is a good rule. It is wise to live a balanced and varied life without permitting anyone or anything to enslave us.

That we must learn to distinguish between the important and the unimportant. Then trifles will not trip us up and we can devote our lives to the meaningful and the significant.

That there is no time like the present for putting into effect the seasoned wisdom of our years. It is now or never if we are to avoid an old age of regret and remorse.

That the man who aligns his life with the good and true need fear no evil.

O<small>F ALL</small> the commentaries on the Scriptures," wrote John Donne, "good examples are the best."

In practicing the art of parenthood an ounce of example is worth a ton of preachment.

Our children are watching us live, and what we *are* shouts louder than anything we can say.

When we set an example of honesty our children will be honest.

When we encircle them with love they will be loving.

When we practice tolerance they will be tolerant.

When we demonstrate good sportsmanship they will be good sports.

When we meet life with laughter and a twinkle in our eye they will develop a sense of humor.

When we are thankful for life's blessings they will be thankful.

When we express friendliness they will be friendly.

When we speak words of praise they will praise others.

When we confront failure, defeat and misfortune with a gallant spirit they will learn to live bravely.

When our lives affirm our faith in the enduring values of life they will rise above doubt and skepticism.

When we surround them with the love and goodness of God they will discover life's deeper meaning.

When we set an example of heroic living they will be heroes.

Don't just stand there pointing your finger to the heights you want your children to scale. *Start climbing and they will follow!*

THE ART OF
Simplicity

SIMPLICITY, simplicity, simplicity!" wrote Thoreau. "I say let your affairs be as one, two, three and not as a hundred or a thousand."

The art of simplicity is simply to *simplify* . . .

Simplicity avoids the superficial, penetrates the complex, goes to the heart of the problem and pinpoints the key factors.

Simplicity does not beat around the bush. It does not take winding detours. It follows a straight line to the objective. Simplicity is the shortest distance between two points.

Simplicity does not elucidate the obscure, it emphasizes the obvious.

Simplicity solves problems. Listen to the testimony of Charles Kettering, a genius of modern research: "*The problem when solved will be simple.*"

Simplicity discovers great ideas; a swinging cathedral lamp inspired the pendulum, watching a tea kettle led to the steam engine, a falling apple revealed the law of gravitation.

Simplicity is a mark of greatness. "To be simple is to be great," wrote Emerson. Only little men pretend; big men are genuine and sincere.

Simplicity has given all the big things little names: dawn, day, hope, love, home, peace, life, death.

Simplicity is eloquent: it is the Twenty-third Psalm and the Gettysburg Address.

Simplicity uses little words. It practices the wisdom of Lincoln, who said, "Make it so simple a child will understand; then no one will misunderstand."

Simplicity deepens life. It magnifies the simple virtues on which man's survival depends: humility, faith, courage, serenity, honesty, patience, justice, tolerance, thrift.

Simplicity is the arrow of the spirit!

THE ART OF
Memory

Tomorrow's memory depends upon today's impressions. The art of memory is seeking impressions which will enrich your life. It is the art of remembering what will *help* and forgetting what will *hinder*.

Your memory builds your personality, your personality builds your character, and your character determines your destiny.

Memory is an art gallery in which you can collect beauty. You can say with Emerson, "The landscape belongs to me!"—and so it does, no matter who owns the land. Through memory you can possess the world and all its beauty!

Memory is a mental bank account. In it you can deposit the treasure of man's mind so that you can withdraw hope, faith and courage in your time of need. You can be a mental millionaire!

Memory is a record of your personal experience. It is a record of trial and error, defeat and success. Past failures will warn you against repeating them. Past victories will inspire you to set new marks of achievement. Through memory you can focus the things you've learned in the past on the life you are living today.

Memory is your link with the centuries. All that men have remembered and set down in print through the ages is a precious legacy to you. The miracle of memory gives continuity to life.

Memory is a form of immortality. Those you remember never die. They continue to walk and talk with you; their influence is with you always.

Memory is something you create for others. "If you make your children happy now," wrote Kate Douglas Wiggin, "you'll make them happy twenty years from now by the memory of it." The quality of your life will determine the memories others will have of you.

Memory keeps the past alive; and a good past is a bundle of todays well lived.

"Memory," wrote Jean Paul Richter, "is the only paradise from which we cannot be driven."

THE ART OF
Words

THE DICTIONARY is full of words. It is how words are *used* that makes the big difference. Words can lift us into heaven or lower us into hell . . . "Good words anoint a man, ill words kill a man," wrote John Florio.

Words sung in a lullaby can put a babe to sleep; words of hatred and passion can arouse a mob to violence.

Words have both the explosive power of a nuclear bomb and the soothing effect of oil on troubled waters. They can start a war or they can keep the peace.

The art of words is to use them creatively; to select and arrange them to inspire the mind, stir the heart, lift the spirit . . .

Words of encouragement fan the spark of genius into the flame of achievement. Legend tells us that Lincoln's dying mother called her small son to her bedside and whispered, "Be somebody, Abe!"

Words are magnets that draw back to us the thoughts they express. "Beware, beware!" warned the Hindu mystic. "What goes forth from you will come back to you."

Words are the pegs on which we hang creative ideas. We must put our dreams into eloquent words that others may be persuaded to help us build them into realities. This proverb of Solomon says it well: "A word fitly spoken is like apples of gold in a setting of silver."

Words of faith, hope and courage lift men upward. Negative words drag men downward. "Nerve us up with incessant affirmatives," counseled Emerson; "don't waste yourself in rejection, nor bark against the bad, but chant the beauty of the good. When that is spoken which has a right to be spoken, the chatter and the criticism will stop."

Words are symbols of man's finest qualities. Words such as *valiant, radiant, triumphant, vibrant, heroic* . . . These are words to live by!

Words are a dynamic force for changing men and nations. Words of power burst in man's mind with a great light, to illumine his thought and show him the way.

Choose well your words! They will go marching down the years in the lives you touch! 🕊️

THE ART OF
Believing

Aʟʟ ᴛʜᴀᴛ I have seen," wrote Emerson, "teaches me to trust the Creator for all I have not seen."

Believing is a daring adventure into the unseen, it is a radiant faith in the unexplored, the undiscovered, the miracles of the future . . .

There is *magic* in the art of believing!

Believe! Engrave these words of the Master in your memory: "All things are possible to him that believes."

Believe! Believe in the limitless supply of God's goodness. The universe is filled with more wonders than you can imagine.

Believe! Project a mental picture of your goal in life. Believing is a creative force that brings the visible out of the invisible. *You must believe to achieve.*

Believe! An old Latin proverb reads: "Believe that you have it and you have it."

Believe! There is a mental magnet within you that attracts to you what you *are*. Doubt attracts doubt and faith attracts faith. Have faith in others and you will inspire them to have faith in you.

Believe! Ponder the advice of Frank Crane: "You may be deceived if you trust too much, but you will live in torment if you do not trust enough."

Believe! Believe in life's enduring values. Stand up and be counted for the things that count.

Believe! Believe that you are big enough to master any problem; that you can handle life.

Believe! Believe that you can go on growing now and through all eternity. Drive your stake far out in the universe!

Believe! The magic of believing is for *you*. As Alexandre Dumas wrote: "Where is the man who will save us? We want a man! Don't look so far for this man. You have him at hand. This man, it is you, it is I, it is all of us."

Believe! ⊰⊱

THE ART OF
Action

A

RT IS expression; it is mind in action.

First the mental image in the mind of Michelangelo. Then action with hammer and chisel and the emergence of the magnificent statue of David.

Religions, philosophies, formulas, projects, blueprints, programs, plans are inert until action infuses them with power.

The greatest truths of God and the mightiest ideas of man remain static and unfruitful when imprisoned in books and chained to pages of paper.

Action releases truth so it can inspire and regenerate; action releases ideas so they can bless and benefit.

Carlyle defined true art as "the God-like rendered visible."

Your own dreams, hopes, aims, purposes mark time until you start them marching.

The work to be done, the goal you seek, will be achieved only when you get off dead center and make a start. Goethe gave us the magic key: "Only *begin* and then the mind grows heated; only *begin* and the task will be completed."

Your ideas and ideals become dynamic when you do something about them, when you express them in everyday action.

Your dreams come true when you *act* to turn them into realities.

"Art," said Tolstoy, "is human activity having as its purpose the transmission to others of the highest and best feeling to which we have risen."

Action sculptures your life; action sculptures the world. You practice the art of action when you act to bring the good into visibility.

THE ART OF
Love

THE SPECTRUM of love merges and focuses all of the arts of living.

Friendship, awareness, happiness, *all of the arts of the good life,* are brilliant beads strung on the golden cord of love.

Love is the foundation and the apex of the pyramid of our existence.

Love is the "affirmative of affirmatives"; it enlarges the vision, expands the heart.

Love is the dynamic motivation behind every worthy purpose; it is the upward thrust that lifts men to the heights.

Love is the creative fire, the inspiration that keeps the torch of progress aflame.

Love penetrates the mysteries of life. "Anything," said George Washington Carver, "will give up its secrets if you love it enough."

Love is the dove of peace, the spirit of brotherhood; it is tenderness and compassion, forgiveness and tolerance.

Love is the supreme good; it is the overflowing life, the giving of ourselves to noble ends and causes.

Love is down to earth and it reaches to the highest star; it is the valley of humility and the mountaintop of ecstasy.

Love is the spiritual magnetism that draws men together for the working of miracles. "Ten men banded together in love," wrote Carlyle, "can do what ten thousand separately would fail in."

Love is the perfect antidote that floods the mind to wash away hatred, jealousy, resentment, anxiety and fear.

Love alone can release the power of the atom so it will work for man and not against him.

Love, in the words of the Master, is the shining commandment: LOVE ONE ANOTHER.

The art of love is God at work through you.

WILFERD A. PETERSON *was born in Whitehall, Michigan, and spent his boyhood in Muskegon. He is now a long-time resident of Grand Rapids, where he is vice-president and creative director of an advertising firm, the Jaqua Company.*

Mr. Peterson is the author of several books, including the best-selling first volume of The Art of Living. *He is a frequent contributor to* This Week *magazine and* Reader's Digest *and is a popular lecturer.*